D1580062

DUBLIN NORTHWARDS IN THE 1950s

Gaius Sutton and Keith Smith

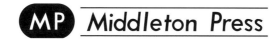
MP Middleton Press

Cover pictures:
Front cover: Details under picture 7.9.
Back cover: Details under picture 4.21.

Published July 2008

ISBN 978 1 906008 31 4

© *Middleton Press, 2008*

Design Deborah Esher
Typesetting Barbara Mitchell

Published by
    Middleton Press
    Easebourne Lane
    Midhurst
    West Sussex
    GU29 9AZ
Tel: 01730 813169
Fax: 01730 812601
Email: info@middletonpress.co.uk
www.middletonpress.co.uk

Printed & bound by Biddles Ltd, Kings Lynn

INTRODUCTION

Some years ago while visiting a well known haunt of mine, the branch line from Gamtoos to Patensie in Eastern Cape of South Africa, the loco left the rails due to a landslide near Togo Halt.

I was given hospitality for the night in a nearby farm together with another passenger Dr Vic Mitchell. The upshot was that he encouraged me to write my recollections of ten days spent on Irish Border trains in 1957. All my photographs in this album are from July of that year and some of the tickets show the date.

My objective was to visit some of those lines threatened with closure partly due to the cost of border customs viz. parts of the Great Northern Railway (Ireland), the whole of the County Donegal Railway including the Letterkerry Railway, the Sligo Leitrim & Northern Counties and the Cavan & Leitrim, the latter now absorbed into the Coras Iompair Eireann. All these and more closed within three years.

I had very little cash, an Ensign single shutter speed camera giving twelve snaps to the film and five rolls of 120 film. My first visit on the Monday after arrival on Saturday at North Wall, was to the GNR Hill of Howth line.

There were two gauges in Ireland, broad 5ft 3ins and narrow 3ft 0ins, these contrasting with British standard gauge of 4ft 8½ ins. On my expedition, all were broad gauge except the County Donegal (with the Letterkerry Railway) and the Cavan & Leitrim Railway.

All the broad gauge lines were part of the Great Northern Railway, except the line from Enniskillen to Collooney, which was the Sligo Leitrim & Northern Counties Railway and the line from Colloney to Sligo, which was CIE (over which the SLNCR had running powers).

During my travels, I was always afforded the upmost courtesy particularly by the then secretary of the CDRJC at Stranorlar.

I am grateful to my daughter, Cherith M. Sutton, for drawing the route diagrams and to my son, Andrew G. Sutton, for scanning my precious album; to my co-author, Keith Smith, for his help and encouragement to tell my story and for seeking out, with the assistance of Hugh Davies, other illustrations from this period to supplement my own photographs. I am also grateful to Hugh Ballantyne who provided much additional information and Norman Langridge for kindly undertaking proof reading.

Gaius Sutton, May 2008

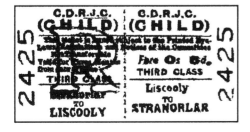
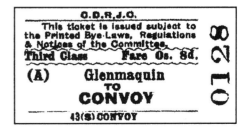

CONTENTS

Route of the journey area.

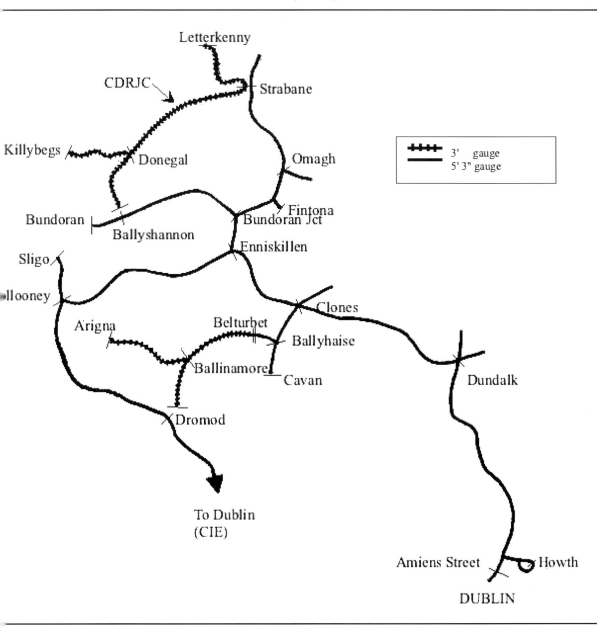

1. Dublin to Dundalk

DUBLIN
AMIENS STREET

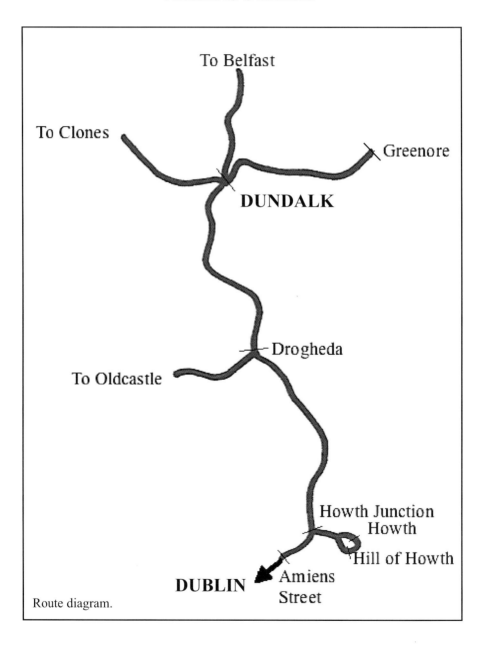

Route diagram.

1.1   We start our tour under the impressive roof. Twin diesel railcar G is waiting to leave for Howth Junction on 1st February 1957. Note the white metal square denoting the last vehicle instead of a tail lamp. This system is still used extensively in India and Africa.
(N.Simmons/Photos from the Fifties coll.)

1.2   Class S2 4-4-0 no. 191 *Croagh Patrick* is entering Amiens Street on 19th March 1959 with the 8.15 from Belfast. The passenger services from Dublin to Belfast were operated jointly by the GNR(I) and the CIE. This line forms the major part of the network which survives, but the Dublin terminus has been renamed Connolly. (R.M.Casserley)

1.3   Amiens Street Shed was photographed on 16th April 1955. The locos shown here were for
the extensive network of the GNR. (H.C.Casserley)

HOWTH JUNCTION

1.4   The Junction is seen on 13th March 1956, looking south from the down branch platform. Here the line from Howth trails into the main Belfast-Dublin line.(H.B.Priestley/Milepost 92½)

1.5   Class T2 4-4-2T no. 2 waits with the 6.15 to Amiens Street on the 25th April 1955. The Howth line survives as part of DART (Dublin Area Rapid Transit), a modern electric network. (H.C.Casserley)

HILL OF HOWTH TRAMWAY

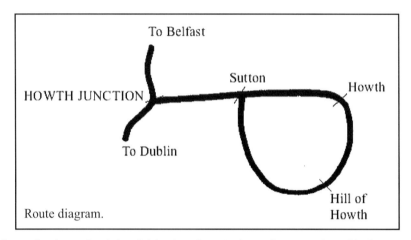

To Belfast

Sutton

HOWTH JUNCTION

Howth

To Dublin

Hill of
Howth

Route diagram.

1.6   The station is on the right of this view from 25th April 1955. The Hill of Howth Tramway was part of the GNR (I). Car no. 8 was one of eight built by Brush with two Westinghouse motors on Brill bogies and delivered for the opening of the tramway in 1901. Edmondson type tickets were issued at Amiens Street for the Hill of Howth line. (H.C.Casserley)

1.7   The tramway joined two stations on the Howth branch, Sutton and Howth, (the bottom loop on the diagram) climbing over the Hill of Howth. Here a car descends to Howth. (Dr. G.Sutton)

1.8   This is the Howth Post Office stop on 22nd September 1957 with car no. 9 calling. This was one of two cars built by G.F.Milnes in 1902, with 40hp motors. Intermediate halts were served and tickets were issued on the tram. They were of small stiff paper, highly coloured bus-type tickets, issued from the conductor's hand held rack. (H.Davies/Photos from the Fifties)

1.9   Trams for Howth and Sutton are seen at Summit station. The wooden keys were inside the rails in the chairs. The Blagdon branch of the GWR in Somerset had a similar unconventional system. (Dr. G.Sutton)

1.10   With full maintenance works at Sutton, it is a great pity that the line was abandoned so early. A few years later, it might have been preserved. (H.Davies/Photos from the Fifties)

DUNDALK

1.11   Class S 4-4-0 no. 170 *Errigal* is seen with the 12 noon Belfast to Dublin train on 18th April 1953. Dundalk was a busy station with a reasonable service to Dublin and Belfast as well as trains working west to Clones and beyond. (H.C.Casserley)

1.12   We continue on the Bundoran Express, leaving Dublin at 8.45 and reversing at Dundalk. Here U class 4-4-0 no. 202 *Louth* is being attached to the rear of the train to depart 10.05 for Clones. (Dr. G.Sutton)

1.13   GNR JT class 2-4-2T no. 90 is with a train for Greenore on 15th May 1950. This train worked from Clones via Dundalk to Greenore, crossing the main Dublin-Belfast line at right angles, as seen here. From Dundalk Quay station the train ran over the Dundalk, Newry & Greenore Railway to Greenore. The crossing of the main line succumbed soon after. (H.C.Casserley)

2. Dundalk to Bundoran Junction

CASTLEBLAYNEY

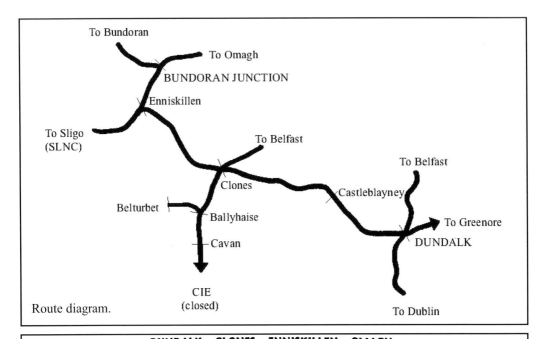

Route diagram.

To Bundoran — To Omagh — BUNDORAN JUNCTION — Enniskillen — To Sligo (SLNC) — To Belfast — Clones — To Belfast — Belturbet — Ballyhaise — Castleblayney — To Greenore — Cavan — DUNDALK — CIE (closed) — To Dublin

---

DUNDALK—CLONES—ENNISKILLEN—OMAGH.

STATIONS	\	WEEK-DAYS															
	a.m.	a.m.	CL a.m.	a.m.	a.m.	a.m.	noon	BC a.m.	a.m.	p.m.	SO p.m.	p.m.	p.m.	SX p.m.	p.m.	p.m.	CL p.m.
Dublin ....dep.	..	..	..	..	..	..	..	8 45	9 0	..	..	..	2 30	4 20	6 25	6 55	..
Dundalk ....arr.	..	..	..	..	..	..	..	9 58	10 15	..	..	..	3 41	6 0	7 39	8 5	..
DUNDALK.....dep.	6 25	..	..	..	..	..	..	10 5	10 45	..	1 30	..	4 30	6 20	8 5	8 15	..
Kellybridge ...... »	..	..	..	..	..	..	..	..	..	..	..	..	..	6 28	..	..	..
Inniskeen .... »	6 36	..	..	..	..	..	..	cTu	11 1	..	1 46	..	4 45	6 34	8 21	8 31	..
Blackstaff .... »	..	..	..	..	..	..	..	..	11 6	..	1 52	..	4 50	6 39	8 27	8 36	..
Culloville .... »	6 46	..	..	..	..	..	..	cF	11 12	..	1 58	..	4 56	6 45	8 33	8 42	..
Castleblayney.....arr.	6 57	..	..	..	..	..	..	10 39	11 22	..	2 11	..	5 7	6 56	8 43	8 52	..
Monaghan (k) .. »	..	..	..	..	..	..	..	..	12k30	..	..	..	..	..	9k30	9k40	..
Ballybay ....dep.	7 10	..	..	..	..	..	..	10 52	11 40	..	2 24	..	5 24	7 24	9 3	9 12	..
Monaghan Road... »	arr.	..	..	..	..	..	..	..	11 51	..	2b33	..	5 34	7b38	9 13	9 22	..
Newbliss........ »	..	..	..	..	..	..	..	..	12 2	..	2b47	..	5 47	7b50	9 22	9 32	..
Clones........arr.	..	..	..	..	..	..	..	cW	12 10	..	2b55	..	5 55	7b58	9 32	9 40	..
» ....dep.	..	..	7 50	..	Runs 1st June to 15th August only.	..	11 0	11 17	12 40	2*55	..	..	6 20	..	..	..	9*45
Newtownbutler ..arr.	..	..	7 58	..		..	11 7	11 50	12 48	3* 3	Stop	..	6 28	Stop	Runs until 22nd June only.	Commences 24th June.	9*53
» ....dep.	..	..	8 4	..		..	11 10	..	12 59	3* 7	..	..	6 38	..			10* 0
Lisnaskea .... »	..	..	8 16	..	Runs 1st July to 7th September only.	..	11 20	..	1 11	3*19	..	..	6 50	..			10*12
Maguiresbridge... »	..	..	8 22	..		..	11 24	..	1 17	3*24	..	..	6 56	..			10*18
Lisbellaw........ »	..	..	8 29	..		..	11 27	..	1 24	3*31	..	..	7 3	..			10*25
Enniskillen......arr.	..	..	8 37	..		..	11 37	..	1 32	3*39	..	..	7 11	..			10*33
» ....dep.	..	7 15	8*45	9 25	11 10	..	12 0	..	2 5	p.m.	3 50	6 40	..	7e40			..
Gortaloughan.... »	..	..		..	..	..	..	BUNDORAN EXPRESS Runs during June, July and Aug. only.	..	..	..	..	..	..			..
Ballinamallard .... »	..	7 26	8*57	9 37	11 21	..	12 11		2 18	Runs 1st June to 7th September only.	4 3	6 53	..	7e51			..
Bundoran Junction arr.	..	7 31	9* 2	9 42	11 26	..	12 16		2 23		4 8	6 58	..	7e56			..
» ....dep.	..	7 32	Runs to Bundoran.	9 43	..	..	12 23		2 36		4 10	7 3	..	..			..
Trillick .... »	..	7 36		9 46	..	..	12 27		2 40		4 14	7 9	..	..			..
Dromore Road ... »	..	7 45		9 54	..	..	12 35		2 48		4 24	7 19	..	..			..
Fintona ....arr.	..	8 10		10 20	..	..	1 0		3 15		4 55	7 48	..	..			..
» ....dep.	..	7 35		9 45	..	..	12 25		2 40		4 15	7 15	..	..			..
Fintona Junction.. »	..	7 55		10 5	..	..	12 47		2 59		4 38	7 36	..	..			..
OMAGH ....arr.	..	8 7		10 17	..	..	1 0		3 11		4 50	7 48	..	..			..
Omagh ....dep.	..	8 20	..	10 35	..	..	1 33	..	4 6	..	5 20	9 59	..	..	..	..	..
Londonderry ....arr.	..	9 20	..	11 35	..	..	2 45	..	5 5	..	6 45	10 55	..	..	..	..	..

*One Class only. a—Calls on request only. b—Will not run beyond Ballybay from 3rd June to 2nd September inclusive. BC—Buffet Car, Dublin to Clones. cF—Calls on Fridays. CL—Calls at certain public road level crossings on request. cTu—Calls on Tuesdays. cW—Calls on Wednesdays. e—Runs 1st July to 2nd September only. g—Calls on Mondays and Dundalk Fair Days. k—Road Omnibus from Castleblayney. SO—Saturdays only. SX—Saturdays excepted.

2.1   This was once the junction for Armagh via Keady and was reached by the Burndoran Express at 10.39. GNR buses are seen in the station yard. Some trains made a connection by bus to Monaghan. (Dr. G.Sutton)

CLONES

2.2   Class Ps 4-4-0 no. 72 makes a fine sight with the 12.45 to Cavan on 18th April 1955. (H.C.Casserley)

May 1953

DUNDALK, ENNISKILLEN, OMAGH, and LONDONDERRY

Miles	Down	Week Days							Sn
	Amiens St.	Y	P	a.m	p.m	p.m	pm	p.m	J
	DUBLIN.........dep	7S30	8 45	9 R0	S	2R45	E	6R20	10 0
—	Dundalk..........dep	8X45	10 5	1045	1 30	4 25	620	8	1121
18	Castleblayney.....arr	9X32	Yy	1122	2 10	5 3	656	8 38	1154
24½	Ballybay...........''	9X49	Zz	1143	2 24	5 24	719	9 5	1210
39½	Clones............''	10X28	1115	1212	..	5 56	..	9 38	1237
52	Monaghan........''	..	..	1 23	..	6 39	..	..	..
68½	Armagh..........''	..	..	2 37	..	7 53	..	..	..
54½	Cavan............''	11 8	..	1X20	..	6 45	..	..	..
53½	Maguiresbridge...''	11 20	..	1 33	..	6 58	10X18	..	..
62	Enniskillen........''	11 37	..	1 48	..	7 13	10X33	..	..
70	Bundoran Junction ''	12 16	..	2 28	..	..	..	..	..
101½	BALLYSHANNON ..arr	..	1 45	3 56	..	..	..	..	2 45
105½	BUNDORAN..........''	..	2 0	4 17	..	..	..	..	2 58
81	Fintona Junction ..arr	12 47	..	2 59	..	..	..	..	..
81½	Fintona...........arr	1 0	..	3 15	..	..	..	..	..
87½	Omagh............arr	1 43	..	3 11	..	..	..	..	..
106½	Strabane..........'	2 12	..	4 41	..	..	..	..	..
121½	Londonderry P...''	2 55	..	5 5	..	..	..	..	..

Up	Week Days						Sn
Foyle Road	a.m	a.m	a.m	p.m	Y	D	p.m	H
Londonderry ......dep	..	..	6 55	S	9S25	9S25	1 25	H
Strabane............'	..	..	7 38	..	9S54	9S54	2 1½	..
Omagh ....''	..	..	8 25	..	10S50	10S50	3 25	..
Fintona ....dep	..	..	8 20	..	10S45	10S45	3 20	..
Fintona Junction...dep	..	..	8 37	..	11S 3	11S 3	3 39	..
BUNDORAN ....dep	..	..	..	..	10S 0	12 10	2X25	1 25
BALLYSHANNON ...'	..	..	..	..	10S20	12 35	2X40	1 41
Bundoran Junction dep	..	..	9 4	..	12S30	12S30	4 10	..
Enniskillen........''	..	7 5	9 30	..	1¼15	1¼15	4 35	..
Maguiresbridge.....''	..	7 22	9 48	..	..	..	4 52	..
Cavan ....''	..	7 25	..	..	1X45	1X45	4 50	..
Armagh ....''	..	..	9 0	..	1 13	1 13	4 15	1056
Monaghan ....''	..	..	10 0	..	2 10	2 10	5 10	1150
Clones............''	..	8 20	1044	..	2X35	3 0	6 12	3 45
Ballybay..........''	7 30	8 50	1116	2 35	3X 5	3 30	6 46	4 15
Castleblayney.....''	7 43	9 5	1134	2 48	3X18	3 46	7 5	4 29
Dundalk...........''	8 15	9 40	1210	3 28	4X 0	4 21	7 37	5 2
DUBLIN(Amiens St.)arr	1025	11R15	2 30	5735	5735	5 50	9R25	6 25

B Buffet Car between Dublin and Clones.   D Commences 1st June.   E Except Sats.   H Commences
7th June.   J Commences 31st May.   P Commences 30th May.   R Restaurant Car.
S or S Saturdays only.   X One class only.   Y Not after 30th May.   Yy Calls on Mondays.   Buffet Car.
Zz Calls on Thursdays.   ‡ Saturdays only. One class only.

2.3   The 12.25 to Cavan (one class only) worked by 102hp diesel rail car no. C1 waits with its wagon for passenger luggage. The boy selling tobacco, chocolates and papers was a time warp. (Dr. G.Sutton)

2.4   The same railcar is seen and behind it is the 12.40 for Enniskillen. On the right is the station pilot engine. (Dr. G.Sutton)

← 2.5 It was not difficult to get groups photographed in Ireland and this is Clones station staff on 19th September 1957.
(C.Gammell/Photos from the Fifties)

2.6 This general view of Clones was taken from the low hill at the west end of the station on the same day. Trains for Cavan and Enniskillen are in the platforms. It is amazing that such an extensive junction should vanish shortly after this photograph was taken.
(C.Gammell/Photos from the Fifties)

ENNISKILLEN

2.7   Class PPs 4-4-0 no. 106 arrives with the 10.55 from Clones on 18th May 1950. The signal box is on high ground in the background. Enniskillen was the junction for the last truly independent railway, the SLNCR. (H.C.Casserley)

2.8   A similar PPs class locomotive no. 46 runs in with the 10.50 from Omagh on the same day. When the GNR closed, the SL&NCR was forced to close. (H.C.Casserley)

2.9   No. 44 was also a PPs class 4-4-0, and was usually highly polished; it often worked the 2.05pm to Bundoran Junction and Ballyshannon. (Dr. G.Sutton)

2.10   Enniskillen was the heart of the railway network in the northwest of the GNR. It is interesting that C1 railcar was stabled near the loco shed and clearly shows that the engine is on a seperate unit articulated to the body. (Rev J.Parker/Photos from the Fifties)

BUNDORAN JUNCTION

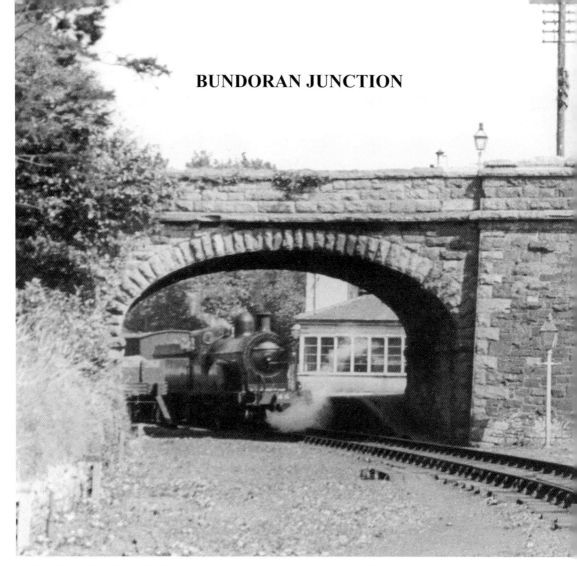

2.11　　No. 46 waits with the 10am from Bundoran on 22nd April 1953. The junction had an unusual platform arrangement, but the Bundoran Express did not stop here. (H.C.Casserley)

→ 2.12　　A view from platform 2 on 3rd September 1957 features no. 44, with an Enniskillen to Bundoran train in the background; a wonderful picture of Omagh, Enniskillen and Bundoran trains which can never be repeated. (N.Simmons/Photos from the Fifties)

2.13   Ps class 4-4-0 no. 73 stands with an Enniskillen to Omagh train on 3rd September 1957, when telephone wires were still on porcelain insulators. (N.Simmons/Photos from the Fifties)

2.14   U class 4-4-0 no. 199 waits with the Bundoran train in the branch platform on the same day. An Enniskillen train is seen leaving the main platform in the background. Note the public telephone box on the platform. (N.Simmons/Photos from the Fifties)

3. Bundoran Branch

BALLYSHANNON

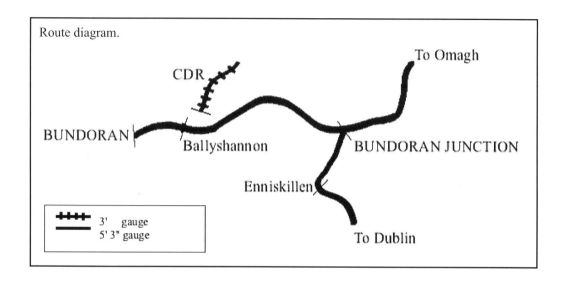

Route diagram.

CDR

To Omagh

BUNDORAN

Ballyshannon

BUNDORAN JUNCTION

Enniskillen

To Dublin

3' gauge
5' 3" gauge

3.1   Another PPs class, no. 50, is at the head of a Bundoran to Bundoran Junction train. The leading vehicle has only four wheels. (Rev J.Parker/Photos from the Fifties)

3.2 Ballyshannon Yard was recorded with a GNR(I) road lorry no. 115, a fairly new AEC. A GNR(I) furniture container is also to be seen. (Rev J.Parker/Photos from the Fifties)

➜ 3.3 No. 44 arrives at Ballyshannon at 3.50. Here we leave the GNR(I) 5ft 3ins system to join the CDRJC 3ft network after visiting Bundoran. (Dr. G.Sutton)

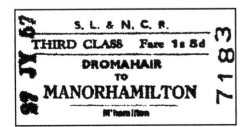

➜ 3.4 This fine westward panorama is from the bridge on 26th June 1958, 9 months after closure. (B.Connell/Photos from the Fifties)

BUNDORAN

3.5   No. 46 is departing from the terminus with the 10am to Enniskillen on 22nd April 1953. (H.C.Casserley)

3.6   An overall view of the station area on the 22nd April 1953 includes the covered platform with a train about to leave on the right in the distance. (H.C.Casserley)

4. County Donegal Railways Joint Committee

BALLYSHANNON

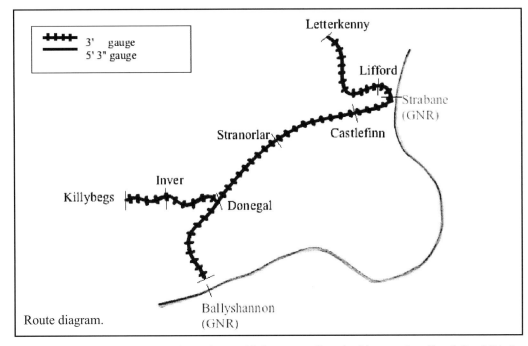

Route diagram.

4.1   Classic Donegal: a rural terminus with its peace disturbed by a noisy diesel. Luckily the passenger portion was articulated and less affected by its vibration.
(Rev J.Parker/Photos from the Fifties)

4.2   A peaceful scene at Ballyshannon, only broken by birdsong. All the components of a railway are present, a signal box, spare coach, water tower and a signal near the turntable. (Dr. G.Sutton)

4.3   Eventually railcar no. 12 arrives from Donegal at 7.02. The signal on the gantry is pulled off. This railcar had a 74hp Gardner diesel engine and contained 41 seats. (Dr. G.Sutton)

4.4   Railcar no. 12 on the 7.10 Ballyshannon to Donegal waits at the spacious platform having been turned on the turntable. (Dr. G.Sutton)

DONEGAL

4.5   The 2.05 Donegal to Strabane is featured in this panorama looking east. (Dr. G.Sutton)

4.6   Two railcars back to back form the 9.05 for Ballyshannon and the 9.03 for Killybegs, both with tall loads of two wagons each. (Dr. G.Sutton)

4.7 The busy goods yard was recorded on 26th June 1958. (B.Connell/Photos from the Fifties)

INVER

4.8　　　There was no passing loop here. In order to pass railcars, one was put in a siding, while the other passed. Seen from a signal, both trains are in the picture. The train in the siding is the 1.34 for Donegal. (Dr. G.Sutton)

4.9　　　The only non-passing railcar in 1957 was the 4.25 to Donegal. This is it. (N.Simmons/Photos from the Fifties)

KILLYBEGS

4.10   No. 12 waits at the platform as the driver poses for the photograph. The train is due to depart at 1.0pm. A fishing boat is at the pier and at that time there were six more tied up further along. (Dr. G.Sutton)

4.11   No. 12 stands on the turntable. Irish railcars were in a class of their own with controls and engine unit at one end only. (Dr. G.Sutton)

4.12   One cannot fail to be impressed by this view of the covered platform which was provided to shelter passengers from Atlantic gales. (N.Simmons/Photos from the Fifties)

STRANORLAR

4.13   2-6-4T no. 5 *Drumboe* arrives at 4.05 from Strabane. The crane here could lift three tons. (Dr. G.Sutton)

Extract from CDJRC Working Time Table 1957.

REMEMBER !

It is well for each Member of this Railway to bear in mind that goodwill based upon years of conscientious effort may be entirely destroyed by a moment's carelessness or indifference toward a customer.

4.14   *Drumboe,* was built by Nasmyth Wilson in 1907 and heads a freight back to Donegal. It left at 4.25pm, Mondays to Fridays. (Dr. G.Sutton)

→ 4.15   The magnificent station was enhanced by its lovely clock tower as befitted the headquarters of the CDRJC. Railcar no. 20 waits to leave for Donegal under the lattice footbridge. (Dr. G.Sutton)

4.16   A westward view on 4th September 1957 has railcar no. 20 coupled to a lengthy train. This railcar and it sister no. 19 were the last railcars supplied to the CDRJC by Walker Brothers of Wigan, in 1950. Both cars were sold to the Isle of Man Railway in 1961 and they remain in retirement there. (N.Simmons/Photos from the Fifties)

4.17   Coaches and wagons were often left by the abandoned Glenties branch platform, as seen here in the late 1950s. (R.S.Carpenter coll.)

CASTLEFINN

← 4.18 This was a border post. The 2.10 freight from Strabane was double headed with 2-6-4Ts no.6 *Columbkille* and no.4 *Meenglas*. It was too long for the siding and so it allows the 2.50pm railcar from Strabane to pass on the wrong side at 3.07. (Dr. G.Sutton)

← 4.19 The freight train then reversed through the bridge to allow the railcars from Strabane and Stranorlar to reach their correct platforms. After departure of no. 10 for Stranorlar at 3.19, the freight came forward again to allow the other railcar to proceed to Strabane. Railcar no. 10 is now in the Ulster Folk and Transport Museum. (Dr. G.Sutton)

4.20   4-6-4T no.11 *Erne* stands with a goods train and is viewed from the bridge on 27th June 1958. (B.Connell/Photos from the Fifties)

RIVER MOURNE BRIDGE

4.21   Railcar no. 12 (built 1934) and trailer cross the River Mourne bridge near Strabane whilst working the 10.05 service from Stranorlar on 17th May 1951. (H.Ballantyne)

STRABANE

4.22   Two gauges are seen at Strabane with railcar no. 20 approaching to terminate as the 11.20 from Stranorlar on 20th December 1954. (H.Ballantyne)

4.23 The company's only diesel locomotive was purchased as a steam engine and re-engined in 1932. *Phoenix* spent nearly all its time at Strabane and is here attaching a van to a railcar. It is also now in the Ulster Folk and Transport Museum. (Dr. G.Sutton)

4.24 2-6-4T no.1 *Alice* is leaving Strabane with the morning goods to Letterkenny on 16th May 1951. The line from Strabane to Letterkenny was a separate railway, but was operated by the CDRJC. (H.Ballantyne)

RAPHOE

4.25 The 12.40 goods from Letterkenny pauses at Raphoe. (Dr. G.Sutton)

LIFFORD

4.26   2-6-4T no.5 *Drumboe* waits with the 3.45 mixed train from Strabane to Letterkenny on 27th June 1958.
(B.Connell/Photos from the Fifties)

LETTERKENNY

4.27   A railcar stands at the terminus on 4th September 1957. Note that the engine cover is open. This was commonly done to prevent overheating. (N.Simmons/Photos from the Fifties)

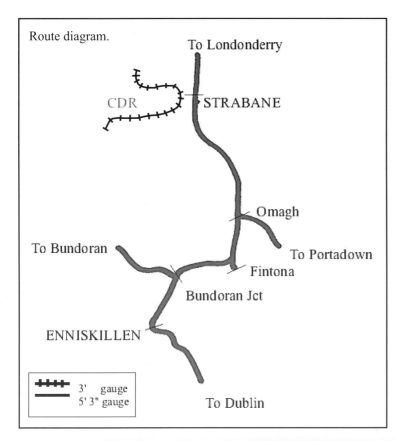

Route diagram.

To Londonderry

CDR STRABANE

Omagh

To Bundoran

To Portadown

Fintona

Bundoran Jct

ENNISKILLEN

3' gauge
5' 3" gauge

To Dublin

Strabane to Fintona

STRABANE

5.1   GNR(I) PPs class 4-4-0 no. 106 is seen with the 1.25 Londonderry to Omagh train on 19th May 1950. The goods crane capacity was 2 tons 1 cwt. (H.C.Casserley)

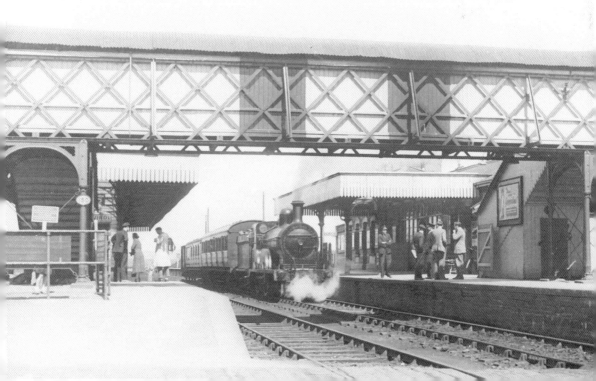

5.2   GNR(I) PPs class 4-4-0 no. 44 waits with a Londonderry (Foyle Road) to Omagh local train on 20th December 1954. (H.Ballantyne)

OMAGH—ENNISKILLEN—CLONES—DUNDALK.

STATIONS	WEEK-DAYS										CL SO			BC	SX		CL SX			CL SO
	a.m	a m	a m	a.m.	a.m.	a.m.	a.m.	p.m.	p.m.	p.m.	p.m.	p.m.	p.m.	p.m.	p.m.	p.m.	p.m.	p.m.	p.m.	p.m.
Londonderry .....dep.	..	..	7 15	..	..	..	9 35	..	..	..	..	1225	..	..	1 35	..	..	3 50	5 30	..
Omagh ....arr.	..	..	8 12	..	..	..	1034	..	..	..	..	1 32	..	..	3 10	..	..	4 50	6 52	..
OMAGH ....dep.	..	..	8 25	..	..	..	1050	..	..	..	..	1 45	..	..	3 25	..	4 23	6 20	7 23	..
Fintona ......arr.	..	..	8 50	..	..	..	1115	..	..	..	..	2 10	..	..	3 50	..	4 55	6 45	7 48	..
.........dep.	..	..	8 20	..	..	..	1045	..	..	..	..	1 40	..	..	3 20	..	4 15	6 15	7 15	..
Fintona Junction.... »	..	..	8 37	..	..	..	11 3	..	..	..	..	1 58	..	..	3 40	..	4 40	6 33	7 36	..
Dromore Road ..... »	..	..	8 48	..	..	..	1114	..	..	..	..	2 9	..	..	3 50	..	4 51	6 44	7 47	..
Trillick ...... »	..	8 18	8 56	..	..	..	1122	..	..	..	..	2 17	..	..	4 0	..	5 0	6 52	7 54	..
Bundoran Junction...arr.	..	8 21	8 59	..	..	..	1125	..	..	..	..	2 20	..	..	4 4	..	5 4	6 55	7 57	..
.....dep.	..	9 4	9 10	..	..	9 44	1128	1230	..	..	..	2 29	..	..	4 10	..	5 5	7 0	7 58	..
Ballinamallard ...... »	..	8 28		..	..	9 50	1134	1236	..	..	..	2 35	..	..	4 16	..	5 11	7 6	8 4	..
Gortaloughan...... »	..	..		..	..	9 44			..	..	..		..	..		..	5 23			..
ENNISKILLEN ....arr.	..	8 40	9 21	..	..	10 0	1145	1246	..	..	..	2 46	..	..	4 28	..	5 23	7 16	8 15	..
.........dep.	7*20	..	9 45	..	..	..		1230	1 33	..	..		4 0	..		6*20		Stop		8*30
Lisbellaw ...... »	Stop	..	9 55	..	..	..		1237	1 42	..	..		4 13	5 11		6*30		Stop		8*40
Maguiresbridge ..... »	..	..	10 3	..	..	..		1242	1 51	..	..		4 21	5 19		6*37				8*47
Lisnaskea...... »	7*44	..	10 9	..	..	..		1246	1 57	..	..		4 27	5 26		6*42				8*53
Newtownbutler ....arr.	7*55	..	10 20	..	..	..		1257	2 8	..	..		4 44	5 39		7* 3				9* 4
.....dep.	8* 0	..	10 24	..	..	..			2 10	..	..		4 50	5 46		7* 8				9* 9
CLONES ....arr.	8* 8	a.m.	10 32	..	..	..		1 7	2 18	..	..		5 2	5 55		7*17				9*18
....dep.		8 20		..	..	..			2 30	..	..		3 0	6 25						
Newbliss...... »	Stop	8 30		10 44	11 0	..			2 42	..	..		3 10	6 34						
Monaghan Road..... »	a.m.	8 40		10 54	11 10	..			2 52	..	..		3 20	6 45						
Ballybay ...... »	7 30	8 50		11 4	11 20	..			3 2	..	..		3 30	6 58						
Monaghan (k)...... »	6k55	..		11 16	11 42	..			2 35	..	..			6k15						
Castleblayney....... »	7 43	9 5		11 33	11 56	..			2 48	3 16	..		3 46	7 13				7 38		
Culloville...... »	7 54	9 16		11 43	12 7	..			3 0	3 27	..		3 57	7 23				7 48		
Blackstaff ...... »	7 58	9 21		11 48	12 12	..				3 32	..		4 2	7 28				7 55		
Inniskeen ...... »	8 3	9 27		11 53	12 18	..			3 12	3 38	..		4 8	7 33						
Kellybridge...... »	8 9					..				3 44	..									
DUNDALK.......arr.	8 15	9 40		12 5	12 31	..			3 28	3 52	..		4 21	7 48				8 5		
Dundalk ....dep.	8 18	10 3		12 21	12 45	..				4 36	..		4 30	8 10				8x25		
Dublin..........arr.	9 56	11 15		2 12	2 35	..				5 50	..		5 45	9 25				9x35		

*—One Class only.   †—Runs fourteen minutes later during June, July and August.   b—Calls on request only.   BC—Buffet Car.
CL—Calls at certain public road level crossings on request.   g—Calls on Mondays and Dundalk Fair Days.   k—Road Omnibus
from Monaghan to Castleblayney.   SO—Saturdays only.   SX—Saturdays excepted.   x—Commences 6th July.

OMAGH

5.3   Q class 4-4-0 no. 123 arrives with empty carriage stock from Enniskillen on 19th May 1950. (H.C.Casserley)

5.4   A line of elderly coaches are behind PP class 4-4-0 no. 76 in 1950.
(Lens of Sutton coll.)

5.5 A wet day and uniforms are a reminder of National Service. (Rev J.Parker/Photos from the Fifties)

5.6 Omagh (North end) (N.Simmons/Photos from the Fifties)

5.7   S class 4-4-0 no. 174 *Carrantuohill* shunts the Bundoran to Belfast through coach on 3rd September 1957. It ran via Bundoran Junction, Omagh and Portadown.
(N.Simmons/Photos from the Fifties)

May 1953

LONDONDERRY LETTERKENNY, DONEGAL & KILLYBEGS—County Donegal Jt. Com.

	Week Days												Week Days								
	a.m	a.m	a.m	p.m	pm	pm	p.m	p.m	Su p.m				am	a.m	a.m	a.m	a.m	p.m	p.m	p.m	p.m	p.m
Londonderry B..dep	..	..	10 0	1 35	..	..	..	6 30	..	Killybegs.........dep	..	..	..	7 45	..	..	1230	3 50	..	..		
Londonderry A.. ⅠⅠ	6 55	9 25	..	1 25	..	350	5 30	6 40	6 15	Ballyshannon... ⅠⅠ	..	..	..	8 0	..	..	12 0	4 0	..	..		
Strabane.........dep	7 45	9 55	1120	2 40	4 0	535	6 10	8 2	1155	Donegal .... ⅠⅠ	..	..	..	8 55	..	..	1 42	5 5	..	..		
Letterkenny....arr	9*20	..	1232	3*50	..	650	..	9§15	1 20	Stranorlar......... ⅠⅠ	645	..	8 45	9 55	..	1 20	2 40	6 5	..	..		
Stranorlar......... ⅠⅠ	8 31	1050	1212	3 32	535	..	6 56	8 40	..	Letterkenny.... ⅠⅠ	..	8 0	..	..	1115	..	2ǁ30	5†35	7 0	9 30		
Donegal.......... ⅠⅠ	9 23	..	1 9	4 30	..	..	7 51	..	..	Strabane..........arr	728	9 10	9 30	1040	1225	2 8	3 25	6 53	8 2	1040		
Ballyshannon D ⅠⅠ	1019	..	2 11	7 E0	..	..	8§45	..	..	Londonderry A arr	..	9 55	..	1135	2 55	2 55	5 5	8 25	9 47	1110		
Killybegs F....... ⅠⅠ	1033	..	2 37	6 3	..	..	8 58	..	..	Londonderry B .. ⅠⅠ	845	..	..	1230	4 0	4 0	..	..	..	..		

A Foyle Road.   B Victoria Road.   D 1 mile to Ballyshannon (G.N.I.) Station.   E Except Saturdays
F Station for Carrick (9 miles).   S Saturdays only.   * Dep. Strabane 235 p.m.
† Arr. Strabane 6 41 p.m.   ‡ Dep. Strabane 8 10 a.m.   § Depart Strabane 8 10 p.m.   ǁ Arr. Strabane 3 47 p.m.

FINTONA JUNCTION

5.8   A panorama facing Enniskillen on 8th May 1950 features visiting enthusiasts. (H.C.Casserley)

5.9   It is September 1957 and this is likely to have been the 4.38 for Omagh crossing the 4.40 for Enniskillen with the connection for Fintona on the left. The GNR (1) always regarded Fintona as a branch. Its railway status can be seen in picture 5.11. The time tables made no reference to the fact that this branch was a tram leave alone horse drawn. The horse was usually kept in its little stable until the steam trains had deperted. (N.Simmons/Photos from the Fifties)

FINTONA

5.10   The tram is leaving on 18th May 1950. Now in the Ulster Folk and Transport Museum, it originally had three classes, First and Second inside, separated by a partition, and Third on top. (H.C.Casserley)

← 5.11   The station frontage is seen in August 1954. We see the massive station platform cover, with brick ticket office and waiting room. The little hut to the right housed the horse between trains. (A.W.V.Mace/Milepost 92½)

← 5.12.   The tram arrives hauled by "Dick". (Dr. G.Sutton)

5.13   We witness another arrival at Fintona. The open platform on the right was not used by the horse-tram. (Dr. G.Sutton)

5.14   We dwell here to marvel at the revenue derived from the conveyance of two sacks.
(Dr. G.Sutton)

5.15   From the First Class leather seats, we look up the line to Fintona Junction. I could not persuade the ticket clerk to issue me with a ticket "They all get on going up" but managed to get a single to Bundoran Junction no. 0410 GNR(I) which I still prize. It was Fintona 10.45 dep. Fintona Junction arr. 11.03.
(Dr. G.Sutton)

6. Enniskillen to Sligo

ENNISKILLEN

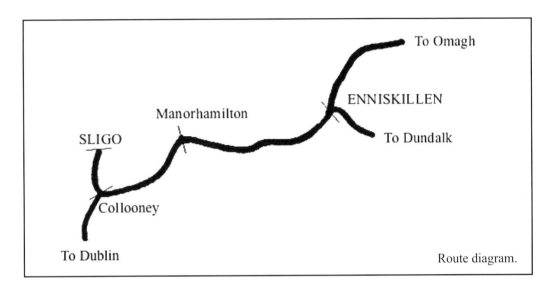

To Omagh

ENNISKILLEN

Manorhamilton

SLIGO

To Dundalk

Collooney

To Dublin

Route diagram.

6.1   PPs class 4-4-0 no. 42 waits with a train for Omagh. There was a crane to lift 4 tons 17cwt. (Rev J.Parker/Photos from the Fifties)

6.2   We are at the north end as a 4-4-0 arrives with a freight train composed of cattle wagons.
(D.Lawrence/Photos from the Fifties)

6.3   Seen with an elevated headlamp on 18th May 1950 is SLNCR railcar A, which had 29 seats. A GNR(I) train is in the background. (H.C.Casserley)

August 1958

DUNDALK, ENNISKILLEN, OMAGH and LONDONDERRY—G.N. (Ireland)

Down		Week Days				Sn	Up	Week Days							Sn.
	B	a.m	p.m	p.m	p.m	a.m	Foyle Road	a.m	a.m	Y	Z	Y	p.m	p.m	p.m	p.m
Amiens St.							Londonderry.... dep	..	..	7 15	7 15	..	..	..	B	1 35	Not after 11th Aug.
DUBLIN ...... dep	8 45	9 0	2 30	4 20	6 55	10 5	Strabane.......... "	..	..	7 38	7 38	..	..	2 30	
Dundalk........ dep	10 5	10 45	4 30	6 20	8 15	1126	Omagh.......... "	..	..	8 25	8 25	..	..	3 25	
Castleblayney ... arr	1039	11 22	5 7	6 56	8 52	1159	Fintona ...... dep	..	..	8 20	8 20	..	..	3 20	
Ballybay ..... "	1052	11 40	5 24	7 24	9 12	1215	Fintona Junc.... dep	..	..	8 37	8 37	..	..	3 40	
Clones........... "	1117	12 10	5 55	7B58	9 40	1242	BUNDORAN ..... dep	..	..	..	7 25	..	12 25	..	1 30
Monaghan ..... "		12b30	6 48		9b40	1 48	BALLYSHANNON "	..	..	..	7 37	..	12 38	..	1.48
Armagh .... "		2 29	7 39		..	..	Bundoran Junc. dep	..	..	9 49	4	12S30	..	4 10	..
Cavan.......... "		12X58	6 46		..	..	Enniskillen ..... "	..	7½20	9 45	9 45	1S33	..	5 0	..
Maguiresbridge .. "		1 17	6 56	10X18			Maguiresbridge.. "	..	Rr	10 3	10 3	1S51	..	5 19	..
Enniskillen ..... "		1 32	7 11	10A33			Cavan.......... "	..	7 40	..	..	1X50	1X50	5 18	..
Bundoran Junc... "		2 23	7A56				Armagh .... "	..	..	8 49	10 0	12 32	12 32	4 57	
BALLYSHANNON arr	1 44	3 50	9A22				Monaghan ..... "	..	..	9 31	1037	1 17	1 17	5 42	
BUNDORAN ..... "	2 0	4 5	9A38				Clones........... "	..	8 20	1044	11 0	2 30	3 0	6 25	..
Fintona Junc..... arr	..	2 59					Ballybay........ "	7 30	8 50	1116	1242	3 2	3 30	6 58	7 27
Fintona ...... arr	..	3 15					Castleblayney ... "	7 43	9 5	1133	1156	3 16	3 46	7 13	7 38
Omagh .... arr	..	3 11	..	..			Dundalk......... arr	8 15	9 40	12 5	1231	3 52	4 21	7 45	8 5
Strabane.......... "	..	4 41	..	..		..	DUBLIN (AmiensSt) arr	9 56	1115	2 12	2 35	5 59	5 45	9 25	9B35
Londonderry P. "	..	5 5	..	..											

A Runs 1st July to 2nd September.   a am.   B Buffet Car.   B Commences 3rd September.
b By Bus from Castleblayney.   H Commences 6th July.   P Foyle Road.   Rr Calls on request.
S Saturdays only.   X One class only.   Y Commences 2nd September.   Z Not after 31st August.

← 6.4 A similar converted road bus left at 12.0 noon from 24th June to 7th September inclusive in 1957. The starting handle remained in place. (Dr. G.Sutton)

← 6.5 This is the SLNCR Enniskillen yard. A railcar with trailer is ready to leave for Sligo. One of the company's 0-6-4T locomotives blows off on the left. (Dr. G.Sutton)

6.6 This general view of Enniskillen is from the east on 3rd September 1957. The railcar in the bay is purpose built railcar B. (N.Simmons/Photos from the Fifties)

6.7 Railcar B crosses the daily freight from Sligo to Enniskillen hauled by one of the Beyer Peacock built 0-6-4Ts on 18th May 1950. (H.C.Casserley)

CDRJC Time Table - Goods trains have been added by hand.

GENERAL TIME TABLE
OUTLINE
(Except where otherwise stated the services named run on Weekdays)

Goods in Ink

Station		a.m.	a.m.	a.m.	a.m.	p.m.	p.m.	p.m.	p.m.	p.m.
				12.40					Sao.	
Letterkenny	dep.	5.20 8.45	—	11.20	2.35	5.30	—	6.57	9.30	
Convoy	,,	— 9.13	—	11.50	3.5	6.0	—	7.24	10.0	
Raphoe	,,	— 9.20	—	12.0	3.15	6.8	—	7.33	10.6	
Lifford	arr.	— 9.39	—	12.20	3.35	6.29	—	7.52	10.25	
Lifford	dep.	— 9.44	—	12.28	3.46	6.34	—	7.58	10.29	
Strabane	arr.	7.25 9.46	—	12.30	3.48	6.36	—	8.0	10.30	
				2.10 227						
Strabane	dep.	7.25 10 0	11.20	2.50	4.50	—	6.10	8.0	—	
Castlefin	arr.	7.48 10.21	11.37	3.7	5.7	—	6.27	8.17	—	
Castlefin	dep.	7.51 10.26	11.45	3.19	5.12	—	6.30	8.20	—	
Killygordon	,,	8.0 10.35	11.55	3.29	5.22	—	6.40	8.30	—	
Stranorlar	arr.	8.10 10.45	12.5	3.39	5.32	—	6.50	8.40	—	
			43	*Sx 4.25*		WSO				
Stranorlar	dep.	8.11	—	12.10	3.45	5.55	7.0			
			Sx 5.31							
Donegal	arr.	8.58	—	1.0	4.35	6.43	7.50		Suo. Noon	
Donegal	dep.	9.5	—	1.35	6.15	8.5	8.5		—	
Ballintra	,,	9.25	—	1.55	6.37	8.24	8.24		—	
Rossnowlagh	,,	9.37	—	2.7	6.47	8.34	8.34		12.0	
Ballyshannon	arr.	9.55	—	2.25	7.2	8.52	8.52		12.20	
		Sao.					Sao.			
Donegal	dep.	9.3 11.15	1.5	5.0	6.46	8.0				
Mountcharles	,,	9.18 11.30	1.20	5.15	7.1	8.10				
Inver	,,	9.32 11.45	1.35	5.29	7.15	8.25				
Dunkineely	,,	9.46 12.0	1.47	5.43	7.29	8.38				
Killybegs	arr	10.5 12.20	2.5	6.0	7.50	9.0				

Station		a.m.	a.m	S.X. a.m.	Sao. a.m.	p.m.	p.m.	p.m.	Sao. p.m.	p.m. a.m
Killybegs	dep.	—	—	7.45	8.55	10.10	1.0	—	3.55	6.40 —
Dunkineely	,,	—	—	8.5	9.15	10.30	1.20	—	4.15	7.0 —
Inver	,,	—	—	8.20	9.32	10.40	1.34	—	4.25	7.15 —
Mountcharles	,,	—	—	8.35	9.43	10.55	1.45	—	4.38	7.30 —
Donegal	arr.	—	—	8.50	9.58	11.10	2.3	—	4.56	7.44 —
					STOP	STOP				
Ballyshannon	dep.	—	—	8.0		12.0		4.0	7.10	10.30
Rossnowlagh	,,	—	—	8.18		12.18		4.18	7.25	10.50
Ballintra	,,	—	—	8.28		12.28		4.28	7.34	—
Donegal	arr.	—	—	8.50		12.50		4.50	7.58	—
								Sn 6 10 WSO		
Donegal	dep.	—	—	9.5		2.5		5.5	8.0	
Stranorlar	arr.	—	—	9.54		2.56		5.52	8.48	
						p.m.		*Sx 7.15*		
Stranorlar	dep.	6.40	8.45	10.0	11.10	1.20	3.0	4.45	6.5	
Killygordon	,,	6.48	8.55	10.10		1.30	3.10	4.55	6.15	
Castlefin	arr.	6.58	9.5	10.20		1.40	3.19	5.5	6.25	
Castlefin	dep.	7.0	9.10	10.28		1.45	3.27	5.10	6.32	
Strabane	arr.	7.20	9.30	10.45	12.40	2.2	3.45	5.27	6.50	
				8.10			*350*			
Strabane	dep.	7.40		11.20		2.35	3.50	5.35	8.10	
Lifford	arr.	7.42	—	11.22		2.37		5.37	8.12	
Lifford	dep.	7.47	—	11.32		2.50		5.45	8.19	
Raphoe	,,	8.7	—	11.55		3.14		6.9	8.40	
Convoy	,,	8.15	—	12.4		3.22		6.17	8.48	
Letterkenny	arr.	8.42	10.10	12.35		3.54	5.25	6.47	9.15	

S20. — Saturdays only; Suo. — Sundays only; S.X. — Saturdays excepted.   W.S.O — Wednesdays and Saturdays only.

6.8   The daily freight for Enniskillen runs in. Note that the last two vehicles were the coaches for the 7.20 Enniskillen to Sligo - an unbalanced working and the company's only locomotive hauled passenger train. (Dr. G.Sutton)

6.9   Looking north on 3rd September 1957, we witness Railcar B on a through working, while passenger coaches stand idle on the right. (N.Simmons/Photos from the Fifties)

COLLOONEY
SLNCR

```
S L & N C R
Third Class          Fare 1s 0d.
       COLLOONEY
           TO
       SLIGO
         Sligo
```
4960U

→ 6.11 The staff pose on 19th June 1957 with 0-6-4T *Enniskillen* as company. It was built by Beyer Peacock in 1905. The SLNCR was unusual in that it never numbered its steam locomotives and they were identified only by names. (B.Connell/Photos from the Fifties)

6.10   Manorhamilton goods shed was recorded on 3rd September 1957. (N.Simmons/Photos from the Fifties)

6.12   Railcar B waits to depart on 3th September 1957. (N.Simmons/Photos from the Fifties)

6.13   The 11.15am mixed train from Sligo Quay to Enniskillen departs on 26th September 1957.
By this time this was mixed only in the sense of returning empty stock to Enniskillen.
(C.Gammell/Photos from the Fifties)

SLIGO

6.14   D7 class 4-4-0 no. 539 waits with the 7.30 to Dublin on 18th May 1950. Note the Gaelic spelling of the notices. (H.C.Casserley)

May 1953

ENNISKILLEN and SLIGO—Sligo, Leitrim, and Northern Counties

Miles	Down	Week Days a.m m	non m	p.m m	p.m	
	Enniskillen.........dep	6 20	12 0	2 0	7 20	..
5¼	Florencecourt	6 33	1213	2 13	7 34	..
12¼	Belcoo	6 50	1235	2 33	7 54	..
17¾	Glenfarne.............	7 5	1255	2 50	8 12	..
24¼	Manorhamilton.........	7 26	115	3 12	8 40	..
33½	Dromahair.............	7 50	1 35	3 32	9 0	..
41½	Collooney	8 15	1 55	3 52	9 25	..
43¾	Ballysodare	8 25	2 5	4 5	9 31	..
48¼	Sligo............. arr	8 35	2 15	4 15	9 41	..

Up	Week Days a.m m	a.m m	p.m m	
Sligo...............dep	6 20	9 30	4 0	..
Ballysodare	6 31	9 42	4 13	..
Collooney	6 38	9 50	4 20	..
Dromahair	7 0	1010	4 40	..
Manorhamilton.........	7 25	1030	5 0	..
Glenfarne...............	7 50	1050	5 25	..
Belcoo	8 20	1110	5 50	..
Florencecourt	8 35	1125	6 5	..
Enniskillen......... arr	8 50	1140	6 20	..

m Rail Car, one class only

➔ 6.15 SLNCR 0-6-4T *Enniskillen* arrives on 18th May 1950, probably with the mixed passenger train from Enniskillen. (H.C.Casserley)

6.16   Seen in August 1954, the station was used jointly by the MGWR and the SLNCR. It had an arrival platform and a departure platform. (A.W.V.Mace/Milepost 92½)

6.17 An amazing line-up on 20th June 1957: MGWR coaches on the left and railcars in the centre roads. An old converted bus of the SLNCR is at the platform on the right, ready to leave for Collooney and Enniskillen. (B.Connell/Photos from the Fifties)

6.18 Railcar B is at the departure platform forming the 9.30 to Enniskillen (operated from 24th June to 7th September inclusive). (Dr. G.Sutton)

7. Cavan & Leitrim Railway

DROMOD

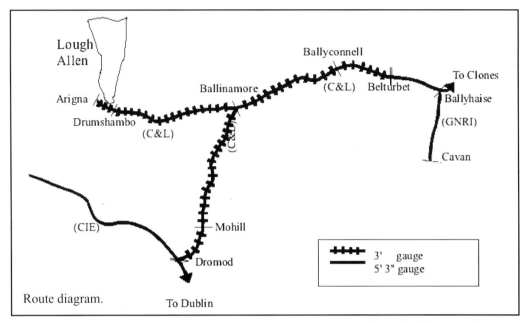

Route diagram.

7.1   4-4-0T no. 2, built by Robert Stevenson in 1887, is seen after arrival from Ballinamore on 21st May 1951. It was one of the eight original C&L locomotives from 1887 and is now in the Ulster Folk and Transport Museum. The original C&L coach was replaced by 1957 by the "bus", which was always on the main line from Dromod to Belturbet. (H.Ballantyne)

7.2   This is the 12.20 to Belturbet on 19th April 1955. The C&L carriage was rebuilt and returned to Dromod in 1953. Two single deck bus bodies were joined and mounted on the frame of a C&L coach as no. 7. This new coach was used until the closure of the line and then sold to Bord na Mona, which now runs excursions over the peat bogs. (H.C.Casserley)

7.3   A beautiful picture features the C&L buildings on the same day. These were separate from the MGW station, although latterly they were not used, tickets being obtained at the MGW station. These buildings are now the headquarters of the Cavan and Leitrim Railway. (H.C.Casserley)

MOHILL

7.4   2-6-2T no.5, ex-Tralee & Dingle light railway, was one of four locomotives which were transferred from County Kerry to the C&L. It pauses with the 12.20 Dromod to Belturbet train on 11th December 1952. An original C&L coach is the first vehicle and the water column on the down line is clearly seen. (H.Ballantyne)

7.5   No. 10 was the only loco with a numberplate and was an ex-Cork Blackrock & Passage Railway 2-4-2T, built by Neilson Reid in 1899. Trains all took water at Mohill, as the water at Dromod caused scaling. Engines working towards Ballinamore had to disconnect and run round to the down line as there was no water column on the Ballinamore line! Hence my picture. Today the water problem persists at Dromod where part of the railway has been restored keeping its name The Cavan & Leitrim Railway. (Dr. G.Sutton)

BALLINAMORE

7.6   This was the heart of the C&L system. We look towards Belturbet on a typical wet day. No. 5 is just coming off the stock of the 12.20 from Dromod. (H.Ballantyne)

7.7.   Ballinamore shed is seen on 1st July 1954 with a C&L loco raising steam. On the left are three other engines, all foreigners, which had come from the T&D and the CB&P. Heading the trio is ex-T&D 2-6-0T no. 3, built by Hunslet in 1889. At closure, there were only four original C&L 4-4-0Ts working. No. 2 is now preserved in the Ulster Folk and Transport Museum, no. 3 went to the USA and nos. 4 and 8 were cut up. (N.Glover/F.A.Wycherley coll.)

7.8   The Arigna branch train is arriving behind 2-6-2T no.5 on 22nd August 1955 and is entering the bay platform. C&L coach no. 5 was always used on the Arigna branch.
(A.W.V.Mace/Milepost 92½)

7.9 Ex-Tralee & Dingle 2-6-0T no.6 waits in the bay with C&L coach no. 5 for the 1.50 to Arigna. Four Traleee & Dingle locos came to the C&L between 1941 and 1958: 3T, 4T, 5T and 6T. 5T survives at Tralee, where a short length of track has been relaid. (Dr. G.Sutton)

7.10 A C&L loco removes wagons etc., from the 12.20 from Dromod after arriving at Ballinamore at 1.30pm. This train was to proceed to Belturbet at 2.00, drawn by 2-4-2T no.10. (Dr. G.Sutton)

BALLYCONNELL

7.11   No. 5, 2-6-2T of 1892 was ex-Tralee & Dingle Railway and it stands on 11th December 1952 with the 12.20 Dromod to Belturbet train. This was the only through train of the day from one end of the line to the other. (H.Ballantyne)

➔ 7.12 Ex-Cork Blackrock & Passage 2-4-2T no.10 is featured as a train of empty coal wagons passes, drawn by a T&D loco. (Dr. G.Sutton)

BELTURBET

7.13   The station had a covered platform for GNR passengers, but C&L passengers had no such luxury. The bus body is, as always, on the C&L line. JT class 2-4-2T no.91 was usually on the short branch to Ballyhaise. (Rev J.Parker/Photos from the Fifties)

7.14   An original C&L loco is seen on a train of cattle wagons at Belturbet. The 4.20 passenger train was headed by 2-4-2T no.10 running bunker first and it waits in the bay platform. Locomotives could be turned at Belturbet. (Dr. G.Sutton)

7.15   2-4-2T no.91 of the GNR is being serviced before leaving with the 5.20 to Ballyhaise. Through passengers had to wait from 3.30pm until 5.20pm at Belturbet. CIE and GNRI made no realistic connections at Belturbet. (Dr. G.Sutton)

Arigna Branch

DRUMSHANBO

7.16   An original C&L loco waits with a coal train for Ballinamore and Belturbet, while T&D 2-6-0T no. 6 takes water from 2.48 to 2.58 enroute to Arigna, with the daily passenger train. (Dr. G.Sutton)

7.17　The 1.50 Ballinamore to Arigna on 17th March 1959 waits for passengers. A peaceful scene shortly before the line closed. (R.M.Casserley)

SLNC Time Table.

GENERAL RAIL TIME TABLE
(WEEK DAYS ONLY)

(A thin line / between the hours and minutes indicates p.m.)

		*R.Car	(A) *R.Car	*R.Car
Sligo	dep.	6.20	9.30	4/ 0
Ballysodare	,,	6.31	9.42	4/13
Collooney	.,	6.38	9.50	4/20
Ballygawley		—	—	—
Ballintogher		—	—	—
Dromahair	,,	7. 0	10.10	4/40
Lisgorman	.,	—	—	—
MANORHAMILTON	,,	7.25	10.30	5/ 0
Kilmakerrill		—	—	—
Glenfarne	,,	7.45	10.50	5/20
Belcoo	,,	8. 5	11.10	5/45
Abohill		—	—	—
Florencecourt	,,	8.20	11.25	6/ 0
ENNISKILLEN	arr.	8.35	11.40	6/15

		*R.Car	(A) *R.Car	*R.Car
Enniskillen	dep.	6.20	12 Noon	1/45	7/20
Florencecourt	,,	6.33	12/13	1/58	7/33
Abohill		—	—	—	—
Belcoo	,,	6.50	12/35	2/18	7/53
Glenfarne	,,	7. 5	12/55	2/35	8/10
Kilmakerrill		—	—	—	—
MANORHAMILTON	.,	7.26	1/15	2/57	8/30
Lisgorman	,,	—	—	—	—
Dromahair	,,	7.50	1/35	3/17	8/50
Ballintogher		—	—	—	—
Ballygawley		—	—	—	—
Collooney	,,	8.15	1/55	3/37	9/15
Ballysodare	,,	8.25	2/ 5	3/45	9/25
Sligo	arr.	8.35	2/15	3/55	9/35

*One class only.

A — Operates from 24th June to 7th September inclusive

Rail Cars will stop at all halts, if required. The 7.20 p.m. will stop at Abohill, Kilmakerrill and Ballintogher Halts, if required by notice to Guard at preceding stations.

C.I.E. Rail and Omnibus Connections at Ballysodare

The 6.20 a.m. ex Enniskillen for stations Claremorris, Athenry, Galway, Ennis and Limerick and Omnibuses, Sligo to Dublin via Boyle, Carrick-on-Shannon, Longford, Mullingar, etc.

The 12 Noon ex Enniskillen for stations on Mullingar and Dublin section and Omnibus to Ballina, Belmullet and Blacksod.

The 1.45 p.m. ex Enniskillen for stations on Mullingar and Dublin section and Omnibus for Galway, Ballina, Belmullet, etc.

ARIGNA

7.18   T&D 2-6-0T no.6 is on the 3.15pm departure with C&L coach no. 5. This is the daily passenger train from Ballinamore. (Dr. G.Sutton)

7.19   A mixed train is awaiting departure on 2nd September 1957. This is the 4.15 to Ballinamore. In 1957 there was a temporary boom in coal traffic, with specials carrying 300 tons each. (N.Simmons/Photos from the Fifties)

← 7.20 The ropeway from the coal mine loading area is seen in August 1954. The boom was short lived for a coal powered power station was built locally, causing coal trains to cease. The line subsequently closed in 1959. (A.W.V.Mace/Milepost 92½)

7.22 Ex T&D 2-6-0T no.4 heads a coal train approaching Ballinamore. The line in the foreground is the main line to Dromod. This study of steam hissing in superb scenery seems a fitting finale to a memorable trip from Dublin. (Dr. G.Sutton)

← 7.21 2-6-2T no.5 is shunting at the mine loading area on 22nd August 1955. (A.W.V.Mace/Milepost 92½)

The Cavan & Leitrim Railway was built partly over the failed Belturbet & Ballyconnell Canal. Sadly the railway has gone, but the canal has been restored forming part of the Shannon Erne link, a millenium project. The author (G.S) navigated this in 1996. The little that is left of the railway evoked fond memories. He also visited the preserved part of the Cavan & Leitrim Railway at Dromod and commends this venture. (UK tel: 00353 7196 38599)